TAKING A BITE *out of* THE APPLE

ROB JANOFF
Designer of the Apple logo

For my parents, Anne and Will Janoff

Rob Janoff

TAKING
A BITE
out of
THE APPLE

A graphic designer's tale

ROB JANOFF
Designer of the Apple logo

Balestier Press
London · Singapore

Balestier Press
71-75 Shelton Street, London WC2H 9JQ
www.balestier.com

Taking a Bite out of the Apple—A graphic designer's tale
Copyright © Rob Janoff and Balestier Press, 2019

First published by Balestier Press in 2019

A CIP catalogue record for this book is available
from the British Library.

ISBN 978 1 911221 61 6

Contents

Foreword

by Joel Bohm

What is it that you are passionate about? Take a moment—it's worth giving some thought, especially when considering a career in the arts.

Throughout human history people have sought fame and fortune. In the past this came about through a heroic act or some remarkable skill. It was harder to achieve for ordinary folk who were often recognized only after death.

Nowadays, "being famous" has become a career in itself. With the advent of social media and influencers, some have achieved an enormous public profile virtually overnight.

Young people especially have a fascination with making it big. When asked, children will frequently tell you that they want to be a famous singer, or an actor, or a race car driver. Big dreams! After all, the desire to "be" something is a shared aspect of humanity's path to identity.

When you dig deeper, what most people seek is recognition rather than fame per se. All humans like to feel they are contributing something valuable through their own, unique input. Few people reach genius level—with commensurate fame—but the pursuit of personal fulfillment drives us on.

When considering what to do with your life, the choices can seem endless. Notwithstanding the need to earn a living and pay bills, it takes time for most people to discover what they are truly passionate about. In the meantime, beginning somewhere is a perfectly sensible place to start.

For my friend Rob Janoff, this was the case. While he was enrolled in a university degree program in Industrial Design, he discovered a new career path, one that immediately captured his attention: Graphic Design. Almost before he realized, he changed his degree and indeed the course of his life.

Of course, you may know Rob Janoff for his design of the Apple logo. While this is still the single biggest project Rob is asked about, he has worked on many others also. His fame has been built on a lifetime of hard work and creative endeavor.

It would be a mistake to assume that the journey to being well known follows a linear path. Some people attain dizzying heights only to drift off into obscurity— their personal capital rising and falling with their ability to garner headlines.

On the other hand, Rob Janoff is a great example of continued recognition, of applied initiative and a great attitude about hard work.

The creative process can be tortuous, but the fruit it yields is both exciting and rewarding. It inspires the imagination and fires up the soul. As you read about Rob's career, do so with an open mind. You will find it an inspiring and instructive narrative.

Not everyone can make it as a creative. Nor is there just one path to creative endeavor, or to making a career with creativity in mind. Use Rob's story as a kind of litmus test. If long hours, frequent disappointments and occasional loneliness while pursuing a journey—that not even you fully understand—doesn't sound tolerable, then the industry may not suit you.

Consider what you yourself are passionate about— cooking, building, acting, accounting… whatever. It's all good.

Don't let yourself be pressured into any career. If art comes naturally to you, then nurture that. Build art into every day.

Oh… and give yourself time.

As Rob Janoff says, "Some of my best projects haven't begun yet."

Joel Bohm
CEO, Rob Janoff Studio
Chicago / Brisbane / Jakarta
November 2018

Preface

This book in the *Hearing Others' Voices* series was written for young people facing the giant, looming question: What do I want to do for the rest of my life?

Unless you are independently wealthy, you're going to have to earn a living, contribute to the world and learn how to "pull your own weight."

To start on your career path, you might as well choose something you really *like* doing. That something is called your *passion* (and you may have more than one). Think about *why* you like doing it—because you'll be spending a good chunk of your life getting good at it and becoming a *professional*. Ask yourself what is satisfying about the work process for you? What is satisfying about the outcome?

My answer to these questions changed a lot of times.

In my early teens, I thought I'd like being an architect for a while—then later, a *landscape* architect. I liked making models of houses with yards, pools, patios and lots of landscaping. However, when I found out what a landscape architect actually *did*, I soon realized how much math and science I'd have to take—not my favorite subjects or where my natural talents were.

When I got closer to thinking about college, I had to get serious about a career. Because of my father's encouragement to find a "well-paying" profession, I initially chose industrial design—designing everyday products for manufacture. I naively thought it was more about designing the *packaging* than it was about designing the product itself.

Well, that career direction lasted about a semester until I got a whiff of what they were doing in the Art Department building, not far from where I was taking classes every day. I finally realized what I really liked was working with words and pictures to tell some kind of instant story. I had always been attracted to packaging and all the graphics involved. So *graphic* design was what I was most interested in—and what I could do best.

All my imaginings of potential careers involved some form of creativity. Not art for its own sake, but art for a *purpose*—something that fulfilled a need. That was the common thread.

Discovering that my "passion" was graphic design lead to a career in design and advertising. Of all the things I could choose to be, a graphic designer, or "ad guy," seemed like the most fun. And who said work can't be fun?

Over time—with real job experience—you learn how to hone your craft. If you get good enough and the right project happens to come along, you might get what is called "lucky." You might get a shot at a game-changing opportunity like I had many years ago, when I got to design the Apple logo.

It all begins with you. You make your own luck by finding and pursuing your own passion. I hope this book—and the *Hearing Others' Voices* series—helps you succeed on your journey.

CHAPTER ONE

A man with an Apple

Silicon Valley, 1977.

The time. The place.

It was a long time ago. Though I remember some things well, by now the details have gotten a bit fuzzy. But I think it went something like the following. At least that is what my friends tell me and how some of the stories out there have it (though, as I will tell you later, some of the tales have it wrong).

It began with a tap on my shoulder.

"Rob!"

I was at my desk at the well-respected Regis McKenna Agency, probably gazing out the window, pondering my project of the moment. Six years out of school, this was my third agency job, and a big step up for me.

Pondering—or what some might call daydreaming—is something artists and writers are prone to do. It's the time and space where creativity happens—where ideas flow freely, percolate, and start to take shape.

I think designers are all like that—they sleep and wake with a project in their heads, or a pencil in their hands.

Yeah, I do remember some bits of it. The magic moment or, as some say, luck—right time, right place. But back then it was just that tap on the shoulder from my boss, Regis McKenna himself.

I heard him say a string of words, but one word threw me off.

"…apple…"

I was still a bit hazy from my daydreaming (or maybe it was lack of sleep), so at first I couldn't make out what on earth he was talking about. Something about apples… lunchtime already?

"Mm. Yes?"

"Logo… logo for a computer."

Ah, a new project. That was something to snap me back.

But this reference to a *computer* was confusing. A computer named *Apple*!? A fruit? No way.

Well, I was young and serious then and near the

start of my career. Little did I know that the logo I was about to create would be recognized all over the world. It would become an industry icon, and the Apple computer would become famous because of... well, because of a lot of things. Incredible.

I put my pencil down, or rather, behind my ear. It seemed that it was a new assignment about something I knew nothing about. So I sat up straighter and started giving Regis my full attention.

I tried to sound firm and with-it (I *was* an established professional designer by then, after all).

"Who? And what?"

"Apple Computer," Regis repeated patiently.

Ah yes! Hadn't he said "apple?" An apple, fruit of all fruits... I loved them.

An *apple!*

I seem to remember feeling the smile rising from my gut, or maybe from my head. It always does when an idea starts taking hold.

Regis McKenna, already a presence in the industry, later went on to do revolutionary stuff, introducing many of the ideas that are now part of the mainstream of technology marketing. He would build a deserved reputation as one of the best public relations people in the high-tech business.

Not someone to be ignored.

Quite apart from what he was about to do for Apple (not that I had any idea of that then), he and his firm were instrumental in launching some of the most innovative products of the computer age. They were the first advertising/PR agency for a microprocessor manufacturer (Intel Corporation), the first recombinant DNA genetically engineered product (Genentech, Inc.), and the first retail computer store (The Byte Shop).

Small wonder he was the one who would soon be peddling the colorful—and true—story of the creation of a new computer in a run-down garage by a couple of rumpled young men, and weaving the tale into our national folklore.

I was incredibly lucky to have him as my boss, a real entrepreneur and pioneer.

Most people thought him quiet and unassuming, but he was already starting, even then, to be called the "philosopher king," the wizard guru who could see his way through the densest thicket. He knew the business and I liked him a lot.

He also knew *exactly* how to get the best out of people. Me included. He was clever enough to discern our different personalities and trot out methods to match.

He smiled and gave me a moment to process the

information coming at me. Being relatively new, we were still getting to know each other. In those days, I appeared "counter-culture"—just by being a bit shaggier than anyone else in the office. But that didn't stop me from being pretty serious about my work, knowing from my previous jobs that I really did have some talent.

Regis knew my "hippie" reputation, but also, they tell me, saw me as thoughtful, a little introverted, a talent worth bringing on. I suppose he'd heard from Chip, my creative director, that I was doing fresh conceptual work on the Intel account.

It seems he figured out that day that I'd respond best to a challenging, unusual-sounding assignment. I guess he was right.

"They're one of the little startups that are all around us right now—lucky for us. Don't know how long they'll last, but for the moment they're our clients. They'll be able to pay, I checked—at the cheap end, of course, but better than nothing."

A computer named "apple"—hmm… that would need a *lot* of pondering.

Regis was aware that what I had done for Intel—the pioneering tech company—was not the usual, expected work for tech trade publications. The Intel ads I created used *non-technical* imagery—fashion illustration, actually—to make everyday, easy-to-understand analogies. This was partially due to the fact that I didn't understand much of the computer stuff myself, which worked to my advantage. It was also my solution to standing out in a trade magazine with its monotonous sea of tech components. I just wanted to look different.

Like every creative person, I liked some projects better than others. Those were the ones that I could sink my teeth into, had a hook for me to play with, and might be fun to produce—the way *I* wanted to.

I already thought that simple was best, and that didn't always go down well with everyone.

"Look, Rob, they're only a mini-outfit, bare-bones really. Who knows if they'll make a big splash in the world... So just knock out something, and make it *look* like it took a lot of billing hours."

Regis treated logo production and design as, more or less, an *extra* service. It just wasn't where his agency emphasis or profitability was. He was more comfortable with the public relations—or PR—end of the business. He took care of his clients and their needs, and always took them all, even the insignificant ones, very seriously.

Regis was the boss—he didn't get that deep into assigning projects. He had the good sense to let the qualified people he'd hired take care of that, and do what they do best.

That's good management—and one of the reasons for Regis McKenna's success. His agency had only been going a few years by then, but it was already making some waves. I was very glad to be with them. I'd only been a few months in the job, but I could tell I was going to like it.

So... I had better pay attention to what my boss is saying.

"Chip tells me you'd be the best one to do it. The Apple Computer thing, I mean."

Chip was the agency Creative Director, so I saw that it probably was a project I'd get credit for if I could make it work. I paid closer attention.

"...Are you up for it then, Rob?"

"Yeah!"

I seem to remember thinking it was a strange assignment—computers called *apples*. I wasn't sure why I got the project. I wasn't really a techie person, and only slightly acquainted with some of our other tech accounts. I could only think it was because I was the new guy and cheap.

"Will there be any official briefing on the project?"

"No, I doubt it... You can ask Chip if you have any questions."

Me, 1976, Palo Alto, California.

I think that I felt pleased by this and tried to hide my smile. I guess he thought the job was a bit up in the air, but to me it seemed, even then, a real tempting project, open-ended and worth tackling. Yes, and as always it *would* need all my conceptual skills, that was for sure. (No designers had *computer* skills back then. Designing graphics on computers wasn't invented yet.)

An Apple computer... hmmm. I began picturing apples in my mind, and all the apples I had ever seen on signs, especially in New York City—"the big apple!"

What kind of apple, color, size...?

What a wonderful lot of things to think about and see, *draw...* Just let me get into it, I thought. Well anyway, that's how I picture myself thinking back then.

I thought a bit more, then I asked...

"Oh, Regis, before you go... who is this *for*?"

"Some guy named Stephen. Says he knows you."

I thought, then I shook my head. "No. He must be mixing me up with someone else."

"Yes, you do. Dark, scruffy, stringy hair, sandals, black T-shirt... Stephen *Jobs*... works in his garage."

"Nope. Afraid not."

Steve wasn't yet that brilliant and difficult genius we think of today, or rich and famous. He was just a young, counter-culture guy like me—wearing jeans and sandals to a meeting while our account guys wore suits and ties. Soon, I would see for myself that Steve—as young as he was and looking the way he did— enjoyed blowing people's minds that he was actually the president of a company.

I was young and weird like him... long-haired and

thought of as hippie-ish, compared to all the account guys in the office. It was that vibe of mine, I think, that got me teamed with Jobs. I was freaky like him, and so I think he trusted me—and I was very happy about that.

"Mm, yes, all right then...," I trailed off and Regis saw that I was already wondering how to get at it...

"Not sure how to start? All right, I'll make it easier. I'll get hold of the visual idea they've been using for the last few months. Ah, I have it here... take a look."

He showed it to me. He must have known it was absolutely useless. But he just smiled and waited.

Before success and fame—Steve Jobs at his garage workbench, 1976.
(Silicon Valley Historical Association)

It was an elaborate, old-time, pen-and-ink drawing of Sir Isaac Newton, who discovered gravity, sitting under an apple tree. Clearly, it wouldn't work, we could all see that. Yes, I realize now that whoever did it was trying hard to project the idea of breakthrough discovery, but my thought was this wasn't a logo at all… but more like an historical illustration. I think it was used as the title page of their first shot at a home computer instruction manual.

Any marketing tool has to be simple and easy to understand… the absolute opposite of this piece.

Not my thing. Not Steve's either. Or his friend and partner, Steve Wozniak's (known to all as "Woz").

"Anything else I should know?," I asked.

"Er, no… Steve just said don't make it *cute*." Cute?… I supposed he meant no corny computer type.

It was all so casual. Here was this new thing. It was going to be a "home computer," as I remember everyone calling it then, and apparently people were going to have this thing at their kitchen table and be able to retrieve recipes and balance their checkbooks. What?! That was obviously stretching reality, I thought, but then that was Steve all over, convinced he could push the boundaries beyond what was possible.

Still for the moment it seemed that my task was to

introduce this idea to the public and make them not afraid of having a computer. I needed to somehow make it look *friendly* so that people wouldn't be afraid to welcome it into their homes.

"Just don't make a 'bug', Rob."

"You mean a *logo*?"

"Yes. No bug. Just do the name in some nice font. It'll do for now."

I don't think Regis—still the tech PR guy—really thought of his business as a full-service creative agency yet—with a design staff. He was accustomed to having clients with just tasteful type treatments of their names.

My gut instinct, then and always, was that there *had* to be a logo. You can't name a computer "Apple" and only represent it *in type*. What a missed opportunity! I decided not to argue the point there and then. I would just do what I thought worked best—and hoped they would get it.

That was the extent of my input from Regis.

He gave me a quick wink and off he went, smiling to himself. I liked working for Regis—you always knew he was really on your side.

It's true... that was the only briefing I got. That would never happen now—but it was all so new and easy-going then. Neither Steve nor I were all that sophisticated.

Steve certainly hadn't yet become that out-of-this-world, demanding guy we think of today.

His only direction had been, "Don't make it cute."

So then, to work.

CHAPTER TWO

Not just any apple

What next?

I decided that the first thing to do was to try to see a bit more into Steve's mind and get a better sense of what he really wanted. It's the same initial part of the process I use today—to see more deeply into a client's real wishes and needs.

Steve, as you know, was a bright guy from the start. Later he grew into the uncompromising visionary we know now—fanatical about good design—but then, he was a free-thinking, geeky young guy. He had a lot of big ideas, but not a lot of experience.

Although I can't personally attest to it, they say that the first thing that hit people about Steve's "workshop" was the smell. The 22-year-old Steve thought that vegans, like him, didn't need showers, deodorants and such. He learned in time though, as you have to when you get famous. Like most of us at that age, Steve didn't know what he didn't know—he just jumped right in and went for it. That was part of what made him so successful. What Steve called his "workshop"—where Steve and his partner Woz assembled their Apple prototypes—was actually his parents' suburban garage. No matter—to Steve it was the gateway to the future.

Steve may have known little about marketing, but he *did* know that the Sir Isaac Newton illustration they were currently using would not do.

Up till then, Apple's visual identity to attract customers had been that pen-and-ink drawing that Regis had shown me. It had been created by Apple's third co-founder, Ronald Wayne—and I'm sure it was an honest attempt to tie in the Apple name with Newton's apple, while also connecting with the idea of "enlightenment." Perhaps Ron felt Apple's name needed some explanation, or added *gravitas*—"Apple" was, after all, an unexpected, frivolous thing to call a computer.

No one knew yet what an asset that name would be.

There was Isaac Newton—who developed the theory of gravity—sitting under a tree, deep in some book, a brook was flowing in the distance, and an apple hovering over him—presumably about to fall on him at a rate of 32 feet per second. Floating around the frame was an unreadable Wordsworth quote: "Newton… a mind forever voyaging through strange seas of thoughts… alone." (What?) The whole thing was wrapped with

The original Apple "logo," by Ron Wayne,
Apple's third co-founder.

flamboyant banners, top and bottom, touting the "Apple Computer Co." This is a good example of the common design mistake (usually made by clients) of trying to cram every idea, trait, product, service—*everything*—into a design—even a *logo*.

But the bigger issue here was the *tone*. At a glance, the etching was real retro—counter to everything we now know as Apple's sleek, timeless beauty and minimalism. And it was the exact opposite of Apple's not-yet-established user-friendliness—your eyes don't know where to go. Perhaps its old-world aesthetic was intended to stand apart from the established tech giants like IBM and Hewlett-Packard, but it totally contradicted the company's message that this new *personal* computer was the amazing, revolutionary thing of the *future*, not the past.

From the first time that Steve came to the office with the prototype for his Apple II, everyone could see that this "logo" was off the mark. Apple II should be branded as the newcomer, breaking out through the frontiers.

It turned out to be a life-changing chance in a million for us that Steve had the sense to try our agency (though none of us had an inkling at the time). I later learned how Steve found our agency; he asked his friend Gordon Moore, co-founder of Intel, who was doing Intel's ads. It was Regis McKenna—and Intel was my account! With the field growing so rapidly, Steve knew that branding a new technology startup in the 1970s wasn't easy. It needed experts like us who already were making some waves for other clients.

I'd like you to picture the scene in Silicon Valley as it was then.

Before it was dubbed "Silicon Valley," the region just south of San Francisco encompassed a few cities, plum orchards and the prestigious Stanford University. Nearby San Francisco had a long history of attracting a diverse population, which included progressive thinkers, artists and intellectuals, as well as the young, counter-culture hippies in the late 1960s.

It was the manufacturing innovators in the Valley— like Intel—that helped catapult the area into becoming the global center of the high-tech industry explosion of the 70s. They developed the game-changing, *silicon*-based integrated circuit used to create the microprocessor and the microcomputer. Imagine the impact—your smart phone would not be possible without it! The nickname "Silicon Valley" now means the same thing all over the world—it's the symbol of tech innovation and scientific development, as well as being the model of a "startup ecosystem," with its cross-pollination of brain-power and resources.

The *New York Times* recently described the 70s Silicon Valley scene as the place "where artists and hippies mixed with technologists, ideas of how to build the future flourished, and a cascade of trillions of dollars was just beginning to crash onto the landscape."

There were literally *hundreds* of companies, entrepreneurs and would-be innovators out there—all struggling to make their mark in the jungle, and advertising their uniqueness in all those computer trade publications. Even though those magazines were full of the tech stuff that could make my head spin, I knew Apple would have to *stand out* above this noise. Steve would need to do something really striking and different if *his* brainchild—not anyone else's—was to grab the attention. And it had to be before anyone else. Timing was everything.

My creative director, Chip, had listened to Steve's prognostications and got hooked. He tried to explain all the benefits of Steve's innovation and how it could change everything in the fledgling category. I understood enough to know one thing... this new Apple thing had to make a big splash.

So it was now up to me. I couldn't wait to get going.

CHAPTER THREE

Taking a bite

I was getting increasingly fixated by the idea—an apple-branded *computer*. What seemed a strange name for a box of circuitry, was sounding more and more intriguing to me.

I knew next to nothing about how this computer worked, so I decided to put that bit aside for the moment.

The easy part of it—what was real for me—was that it was called "Apple." You had a complicated machine named for a fruit, so it was clear what I was going to do as far as the logo went. It had to be an *iconic* apple.

I also knew I had to keep it simple, otherwise it would never be remembered.

But achieving simplicity *and* originality isn't easy. I

had about two weeks for this assignment, so I started to dig in.

I could see right away that I had to look at an apple every which way, every shape, every section, angle, every perspective—and somehow see into the *idea* of an apple.

One fun and friendly apple. I still had no real idea about how I would do it, but—I *knew*.

I knew that it was there, somewhere—an essential apple, there for the picking, waiting for me to find it.

An apple.

I was picturing an apple in all its hues. Red? Green? I totally loved the zing of bright, vibrant colors— vibrating you, pulling you. I knew *that* would make our apple really stand out.

Easy enough to say.

Something more was needed, a different twist, and that could only come from hard work. And inspiration. I just hoped that I could manage that in my final product. In my mind, it was going to be *beautiful*. I so wanted it to be.

My boss had told me he didn't want a "bug," or icon—just an all-type logo. But I thought, gee, with a name like that you *have* to do an icon. I would tell Regis when I had a spare moment that if we *didn't* see the fruit idea—the *apple*—we'd lose all the fun-ness of it. Or better, I'd *show* him.

The briefing on the assignment was really a "non-brief." I've always loved a challenge—but a request to present the right design solution *without* a full brief—I wouldn't *think* of it today. I'd be interviewing the client up and down for hours. But I didn't know better then. Neither did Steve. Maybe that was a good thing. I was unencumbered by too much input and free to create what *I* thought was right. In fact, this logo we all know today would never have happened if I had listened to everybody else.

I realized that Steve and I had some things in common, we were both coming from the same generation and mindset. As I thought of vague directions for this apple logo—nothing concrete yet—I started to assume that Steve would be on my side, that we'd *both* like the direction I was taking.

Not that I had the slightest inkling yet that our Apple would become a mega-icon and the most recognized brand in history, I just wanted to do a good job for Steve. Even more, for me.

I pondered some more. I could see intuitively that I had such a great dichotomy to work with. A brilliant breakthrough, naming something as complex and *cold* as a computer after a simple, living, piece of fruit—something mechanical and something organic. It was wonderfully contradictory.

I never felt inadequate because of my lack of computer knowledge, because I was designing for consumers who *weren't* computer savvy—like me. I'd turn that very thing into an asset. I'd show millions of people who knew nothing about computers that computers *could* be user-friendly, *could* be fun. For their children too. Yes… not all wires, circuit boards and hardware, but fun to look at, to buy, to show your friends, to *use*.

Our creative director talked about the amazing things this little home computer could do and how it could become a game-changer. I'm not sure I quite believed programming home computers for filing recipes and balancing checkbooks would one day become as popular as it eventually did, but that was going to be my goal.

I needed to find a way to put those benefits into terms that anyone could understand—visually somehow.

Yes, that was it. I'd show them the *idea* of a living-on-your-kitchen-table computer—your own Apple friend—not the threatening machines that computers were then. I was going to help change all that.

I felt that the right course of action for me was to focus

first on the *apple*, not on the computer—at least not yet. Steve hadn't called the company "New Technology Systems" or anything expected like that, he had called it "*Apple* Computer Inc." That's what made it different. And besides, I *liked* apples.

I would make the most of it, *play* with it, and look deep into that idea.

"Apple." It figured. Steve had been a fruitarian who had lived mainly on apples (his favorite, you've guessed, was the "Macintosh" variety).

After he dropped out of college, Steve took calligraphy classes, traveled to India, and spent time on a ranch or farm or commune or something of the kind in Northern California where they had an apple orchard. He thought apples were the perfect food. So when he was looking for the best name, "Apple" was the first thing that came to his mind.

The story I later heard about how the name "Apple" came to be was that they had a list of names for the company and they had to pick one the next day to sign business papers. Apple was the favorite on the list and if they couldn't come up with something better, "Apple" it was going to be, even though Woz, Steve's partner, thought they would get sued by Apple Records—the Beatles' label. (We were all Beatles fans in those days.)

They didn't come up with something better, and I'm very glad of that. (They did, however, get sued by Apple Records—but eventually they worked out a deal together.)

The Beatles' Apple Records label.

All right then, back to focusing on the basics.

The formal position (always worth noting) was that I had been selected by the Regis McKenna creative director to design the corporate identity package for Apple Computer. It was because of my hard work for tech clients, he said, and because I was considered to be a *conceptual* art director—able to translate complex hi-tech information into easy-to-understand visuals.

Graphic design is all about *communicating*—it's about *distilling* ideas, things, attitudes, personalities and places into the simplest words and images. To get there, you often need to know more than you need to, achieve more than is reasonable, and bust through endless limits. And, yeah, great marketing connects with people, but you still need to combine it with a flawless product to succeed. All of that takes commitment.

I knew that Steve and Woz were trying to get Apple known as a big new deal. It's funny to think now... two Steves *changed the world* from their garage by making an impersonal computer into something *personal*. It seems incredible that they achieved just that. However great, the product could take it only so far, the graphic communication had to take it the rest of the way.

So I knew my effort would need to stand out to be seen above the clutter.

I was beginning to believe in Steve. *His* commitment was obvious. And I was committed to making a success of this assignment.

So back to my obsessing... *Think*! What can you do with an apple!

And this time *look*.

I went out to the nearest produce store and bought

a bunch of apples. Then I put them on my table, and started to draw them.

It was like ninth grade art class, where I had to render a bell pepper over and over. Just like that, I tried to get a generic apple shape, figuring out what made an apple... an *apple*. There's the shape to it, and the stem and the

leaf, which apples don't always have but people imagine they do. I stylized them into a kind of generic silhouette, the shape that so instantly read "apple".

I kept working on this for several days. Hour by hour, I was simplifying the shape till I had gotten an easily recognizable silhouette.

Well, now I had a fruit. A round fruit.

It was beautiful, but somehow... a bit ordinary. It didn't seem, even to me, to be specifically an apple. It might even be seen as a cherry.

I kept drawing it intuitively. I went on doodling

around, shading it in and so on, really enjoying myself. I tried looking at my drawing every which way.

The shape was better now. But it was definitely not striking enough for a *logo*. People would just see an ordinary round fruit (well, not exactly round), and go on past it because there was nothing special about it to pull them to it, nothing *arresting* that had any kind of *surprise* about it. I knew that it would never make a mark—not unique enough, or *true* enough.

I concluded, sadly, that it was a false start. Designers sometimes have to go through that—but hopefully they don't give up.

I decided to try something else.

What else can you do with a fruit? Or more to the point, with an apple?

Ah. You cut it up, don't you?

I went back to the store and bought another bag of apples.

This time I would try getting inside them—would *that* lead to anything? After all, the core of an apple is *inside*, so maybe there's where I would reveal its essence—the key I had to find.

Then I sliced one in half vertically... Eureka!

Right there and then I discovered that classic apple shape I was trying to get. So graphic. The perfect outline silhouette of an apple.

Better. But it's still *just* an apple. Nothing special about it.

Besides, what else could it look like? Couldn't this be a cherry? They both are round with their distinguishing top and bottom curves—or what I call their "shoulders and feet."

I pored over the outline again. It still seemed ordinary, as if there was nothing to grab onto, much less anything that could signify a new brand, or stand out from its surroundings, something a logo *must* do.

Still it was all I had to go with. I wasn't ready to rethink and start over, as designers sometimes have to do. So I just went deeper.

Let me start from the human experience. What do you *do* with an apple?

After all that endless thinking, it suddenly came like a lightning flash.

It's an apple, so, of course, you eat it.
Yes, but first, you—yes yes *yes*…?
You *take a bite*.
So I did.
That's it. That's *it*! That's IT!
It's an… APPLE!

CHAPTER FOUR

Ripening it

Finally I was at a place where I could say to myself, "I think I did it."

It was all about scale. You couldn't take a big bite out of a cherry. The bite made it look like an *unmistakable* apple.

And beyond that, the bite invited the viewer into the picture. It implied that you, too, can take a bite of the new world that Apple computers was bringing into your home. It made the logo *interactive*.

When I first showed the idea to Chip, my creative director who translated computer jargon for me, he looked at it and said, "Oh, guess what, Rob. You just designed something you didn't realize. The word "byte"—b-y-t-e—is a computer word. And you took a byte out of Apple." That was just a happy accident.

Chip was laughing. I was blown away!

I wasn't computer literate enough to see that initially (few people were in 1977). Then I thought, "So *there*'s a bit of wit that will last!" Any logo that makes a joke or engages you in that way, you're going to remember.

I like having a sense of humor—I like being able to have provocative headlines and imagery that engage your eye, or your mind, and make people think in a different way. It's a real powerful thing, especially as your work gets more and more exposure. Little did I know that this bitten apple would change the way the world sees things. Although the Apple logo has changed a bit over the years, it's still the same basic shape I designed all those years ago.

Once I got the scale of the apple nailed down by using the bite as a size relater, I needed to make this apple different and *really* stand out. For this I went into the Apple—not the fruit, but the *computer*. I figured the thing that made this computer special is what would make my logo look special.

The "USP," or *Unique Selling Proposition*, of the Apple II was its ability to show computer images *in color* on your home TV. While other computers came with their own black and white monitors, the first Apple didn't require a separate monitor (though one was available in black and white). Instead, it could use the color capabilities of your TV at home. At that time, color TVs used a test pattern of colors—shown on screens as stripes or bars—that was used to adjust the hues whenever the TV picture was too red, blue, or whatever.

That's it! This apple won't only be the natural fruit colors of red, green and yellow. The full-color Apple logo will be stripes of red, green, yellow... *and* orange, purple and blue!

It's fascinating to look back at the changes since I came into the business. Maybe my Apple design looked revolutionary for the tech category at the time because the *product* was revolutionary. I soon started noticing more and more color being used in the tech trades after that, but it seems that the very colorful Apple logo was among the first to bring those influences to the category.

I have to admit, at the time I was also greatly influenced by the pop art graphic explosion of the late 60's and early 70's—artists like Peter Max, and movies like the Beatles' "Yellow Submarine."

The day came to present the new Apple logo design to Steve Jobs. Just the one, not any alternate concepts. I did, however, show him the main multi-colored striped version of the logo, as well as solid color versions, each

The bright colors and bold graphics of the Beatles' movie "Yellow Submarine" and the pop art of Peter Max were big influences on me.

in one of the six colors of the stripes, plus even a metallic version.

I would never show just one design concept to clients now, I always give them at least three options. Most clients like choices. They need to like one over the other and feel ownership of the final choice. But it's also important not to overwhelm clients. Editing down to only the few best is the *designer*'s job.

But I showed only one design to Steve then. It was really low-key. He was just starting his career, and so was I, really.

I presented my one or two boards with the one basic design and its variations... and held my breath.

He just smiled and nodded. He didn't say much, that wasn't his style. But I could tell he was pleased. No suggestions. No tweaks.

I didn't have to sell hard or pitch the idea to Steve. We both intuitively liked it and felt it was the way to go. Just... there it was! So I guess he trusted me. It's the only time in my entire career that I presented only one solution. But we both knew it was *right*.

However, I did have a hard time getting the multi-color version out of the agency. One older account person said we were "nuts" recommending it for this little company, Apple, saying, "You don't want a six-color logo—you'll go broke with printing costs." The technology for easy multi-color reproduction wasn't available then. But Steve wanted it to be really top-notch and didn't care about the expense.

So that was that. Steve's spare-no-expense position paid off. Last year, Apple became the richest company in the world with a value of over one trillion dollars.

In 2015, Apple's Chief Design Officer, Jony Ive, spoke to the *New Yorker* magazine about the jarring nature of the creative process: "You go from something that you feel very protective of, and you feel great ownership of, and suddenly it's not yours anymore, and it's everybody else's."

I've felt the same way when I was surprised to come across one of my print ads or TV spots. Even today, it's almost an out-of-body experience when the Apple logo pops into my field of vision unexpectedly. I've heard other creative people say it's the same for them.

I feel incredibly lucky to have crossed paths with Steve Jobs just when I did, and for it to have worked out the way it did. It's kind of like watching your kids grow up and do really well. I'm incredibly proud of my kids—and of my logo too.

But of course, I didn't know all this would come to pass back then. We were just riding the wave and, for the moment, enjoying our success in getting this little startup company off the ground.

In no time at all we were into all-out production: artwork for print ads, signage for the big upcoming West Coast Computer Fair, labels on related hardware and software, logos on hats and clothing—the works! I felt so pleased to be an integral part of the launch of that ground-breaking new "toy."

It turned out lucky for us that the word "apple" has so many positive associations—like "American as apple pie," "an apple a day keeps the doctor away," and New York City's nickname, "The Big Apple."

Apples also have become linked in many minds to that

magical first letter "A" in the Latin alphabet—magical because of our collective childhood memories of our very first reading books and the striking illustration of an apple next to the phrase "A is for Apple." It's our introduction to a world of knowledge and learning— and a primal connection. I was able to build on that association in the first ad we created for Apple.

This was the first print ad for the Apple II, 1977.

I doubt very much if I thought of any of this when I drew that first silhouette. Perhaps it lurked somewhere in my subconscious.

Aside from the aesthetics of it, for me, the idea behind the Apple logo design was always about seeing a familiar object in a new way.

Never in a million years could I have dreamed it would end up everywhere. *Everywhere*! Even more than the mega-brands, Coca-Cola and Marlboro. Even more than Google. I've heard that it's the most recognized image in the world.

But, to go back again to our story, I remember vividly the glorious day of the launch of the Apple II computer at the West Coast Computer Fair of 1977.

There was my beautiful apple logo, right up there for all to see.

And in the jumble of all those massed competitive displays, guess what? The fair-goers flocked to the full-color images and professional branding of Apple's bright and lively booth. And the machine that had just been created by two young guys in a backyard garage started earning millions. It was quite a year!

I often think of the many times I'd heard suppliers from outside of the agency say, "They'll never make it. They're going against giants." Well, they were wrong.

Before long, Apple was having an enormous opening day celebration of its new Cupertino office, which would eventually grow into a campus. The party featured a tethered hot air balloon hovering above the building with a huge Apple logo displayed on it. I went up in that balloon with Steve, my 8-year-old daughter, and the largest version of my design yet.

Apple celebrated the opening of its brand new offices in a big way.

Once the Apple logo design was adopted, and the Apple II computer launched, I got busy working on the Apple II advertising campaign with the agency copywriter assigned to the Apple account (we are still friends today). We came up with the concept of a series of two-page ads featuring famous American innovators like Thomas Edison, Thomas Jefferson, and the Wright brothers—each in the appropriate period setting and costumes, except for the jarring presence of an Apple computer on their desks. The ads pondered how much more they all could have done with an Apple computer! It was an entertaining way to demonstrate all the things you could do with an Apple computer by *your* side. The photo shoot was like creating a theater set with actors and props. Tons of fun for me to art direct. And a fun way to get Apple noticed.

We didn't have any idea then how Apple Computer would grow, not even the famous Steve Jobs. Well, perhaps he might have—it's too late to ask him now. I can just hear him saying, "Wow, oh wow" as he moved on to his next phase of creation. I guess his legacy will never stop.

Steve Jobs launches the Apple II into history,
at the 1977 West Coast Computer Fair. (Science Channel)

CHAPTER FIVE

Golden Apples

In design—as in life—you can't overestimate the power and impact of color.

Apple's multi-colored, striped logo, I believe, was instrumental in getting the unknown Apple computer noticed and off the ground. The stripes showed, clearer than words, Apple's difference from the competition—it could create *color* graphics that you could see on your TV at home. The logo's vibrant rainbow hues highlighted the ability of the Apple II to display a variety of colors, which had never before been a feature of home computers. In the very beginning, there were only a few colors in the palette, which were reflected by the test pattern color bars on the monitor. In short order though, the color capability of Apple computers seemed unlimited. That really was astounding.

While the colored stripes illustrated Apple's main point of difference when compared to the competition, they also served a more important function. One of my biggest challenges in designing the logo was to make the concept of a home computer something *friendly,* especially for kids and schools. Computers back were thought of as massive machines with a cold and negative connotation. We wanted to create a warm and positive feeling about the Apple computer—something inviting for the whole family to use.

I think we did.

There's this idea around that if you make a brand impression during a kid's school years, he or she is yours

The test pattern on an early color TV; and the Apple logo on the new Apple II nameplate—the first time it was ever seen by the public.

for life. The stripes are also like rainbows—which of course seem happy and fun—something kids of all ages can respond to. As I said, I was also influenced design-wise by the graphic explosion and the psychedelic pop art of the late 60s—the signature of a new generation. It was a fun, alive time to be a young designer.

The colors were harder to print back then—each stripe had to be printed in its own specially mixed color, and in those days at considerable expense too. The registration of one color to the next gave printers headaches! Steve was keen on the idea because he knew the vivid colors improved people's *emotional* response. And for designers, I believe, emotional responses are what matters. Steve wanted the colors in, and that was it. There was no arguing with Steve, even then.

Mind you, Steve could be hard to keep up with—that was probably what made him such an innovator and so unmatched. Thinking about it now, I am not surprised that the third founder of Apple, Ronald Wayne, dropped out of the partnership. He said "the Steves" were like two whirlwinds—"it was like having a tiger by the tail and I couldn't keep up with these guys."

The Apple II was not a computer for a graphic designer like me. With the Apple II, you had to know how to program and use computer language. It wasn't

*"The Steves"—Wozniak and Jobs—with an Apple II circuit board.
Check out Woz's belt buckle!* (Silicon Valley Historical Association)

until Apple's Macintosh came along that the operating system changed, and computers became more intuitive and user-friendly—opening the door for designers and other professionals.

The first time that Steve came to see me at the office he brought a prototype of the Apple II—a fiberglass case with clean-lines and curved edges, in an off-white shell.

When the first mass-produced computer was in the development stage, Steve used to wander around Macy's at the Stanford Shopping Center in Palo Alto to look at their kitchen countertop appliances. The fact that Steve found inspiration for the shape of the Apple II by studying streamlined electric mixers and blenders

The sleek look of the Apple II was inspired by kitchen countertop appliances.

still makes me smile. It shows how visionary and detail-oriented he was—a home computer had to look home-appropriate!

The Apple II was an *immediate* success. And so was the logo. It's been over 40 years since that original logo was first shown and I can't even guess how many people have seen it. It is true that the symbol has been slightly revised and nuanced a few times over the years—as was fitting—but it has never been replaced.

It may be stating the obvious, but clearly Apple's overwhelming success is due to Steve Jobs, not to me. Maybe because he started out as a counter-culture young guy who really did *think different.* He had a remarkable insight—intuition really—into what people wanted in an electronic device, even before they had any idea they wanted it. Yeah, he saw what was needed and went for it. And he never stopped coming up with new ideas.

Apple's fast rise was also supported by Steve's incredibly high standards for functionality and design. They were a huge factor. The elegant machines just worked... beautifully.

No question, Steve was a real genius. He's certainly earned his place in history.

What part did the logo play in Apple's success? I have often been asked that. Actually, I think great brands and great logos go hand in hand. A crappy product won't be saved by a great-looking logo, just as a great product with a forgettable brand image won't get the traction it needs to be a success.

So I think the logo did help. Today few companies enjoy the enthusiastic fan base that Apple does, and it seems that Apple's *visual* prowess—in graphics and product design—plays a big role in its successful reputation for industry-shifting technology, which they keep cranking out. It shows the importance of inspired marketing and presentation. Build the right brand, and they will come.

Over the years, Apple logos keep showing up in more and more places.

There are bitten apples tattooed on arms, stickers on car windows, on shirts, hats, mugs, everything! Cartoonists and poster designers use it, pop culture has embraced it. It has become a global icon.

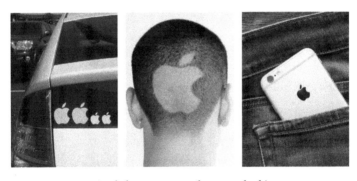

Apple logos—everywhere you look!
(Car: Lenore M. Edman; hair cut: Derek Yee, Octopod Studios/No Starch Press)

Yeah, and they say the Apple logo even makes people more creative! There was an experiment conducted by two academics who subliminally flashed either the Apple logo or the IBM logo at students, while they were performing a "visual acuity test"—they had to list all the possible uses for a brick besides building a wall. The students didn't *consciously* know they'd even seen a logo—it went by so fast—but their answers after

Can a logo make you think different?

the Apple logo was flashed were judged to be far more creative than those after the IBM logo was flashed. That's just amazing. Wouldn't it be fun to see if people could do other things more creatively, beyond finding uses for theoretical bricks?

I've never heard of that phenomenon happening with anything else. I know the Apple brand attracts a certain kind of person, but does it really help you "think different," as their ad campaign of the late 90s suggests? That shows the power of good branding and design.

You're thinking there's more behind the Apple icon?

Apple fanatics like to rationalize the meaning of my rudimentary apple shape with its missing bite, pointing to various allusions—even the biblical story of Adam and Eve, taking a bite of the forbidden fruit of the tree of knowledge!

So many stories have spread about how it happened, national folktales by now, especially all the tales about why I designed the logo the way I did. The stories are way more interesting than my rationale! Stories are told and people believe them and the lore gets passed on (and all this even before social media!). The fact that people believe the stories tells me that they feel a special connection with it, even beyond the love they have for the devices the logo adorns.

After the rainbow-striped gay pride flag was introduced, many thought that the color stripes of the Apple logo were used in memory of Alan Turing. He was the inventor of the modern computer, the unsung World War II hero who cracked the Nazis' military codes, thereby helping to end the war and saving millions of lives. He was later persecuted in England for being a homosexual, and committed suicide in 1954,

Many myths have spread about the "hidden meaning" of the Apple logo, including Adam & Eve, the gay pride flag and computer pioneer, Alan Turing.

they say, by eating—yes—a poisoned apple. It's quite a good story and I could see how the idea caught on, but it was not part of my thinking when I took that bite. The truth is the Apple logo was designed a year *before* the gay flag even came out.

To everyone their own interpretation, and that's good—the fruit (ha!) of a great design. People find their own meanings and have their own emotional responses. With so many of us devoted to our iPhones and Macs, bowing reverently toward the screens, it is no surprise that these creation myths exist.

My aim was simply to get noticed in all those computer publications and stores, which wasn't that difficult in the tech field then. My thought was, as always, to keep the logo simple. The solitary apple, with a hovering leaf cocked to one side, did just that.

The rainbow stripes had no deep mystery behind them either. Besides illustrating Apple's color capabilities, Steve wanted the computers to appeal to children, who could use them as an educational tool. Plus, almost everything else in the tech field was blue, so we put some different colors in it. It was kind of complicated, but eye-catching and a little bit of a counter-cultural symbol, I suppose. Even in those early days, stickers of the rainbow Apple logo were beginning to appear on the back of cars, like a membership badge in a private club.

There have been many other attempts to analyze why the Apple logo has continued to be so loved. One was by a graphic designer who saw the Fibonacci sequence, or the Golden Ratio, as the underlying geometric structure of the logo itself! This was not consciously in my mind at all when I did the design, but—who knows?—maybe it's one of the intuited design choices that has helped Apple's logo endure the test of time.

I like to invite people to focus on some logo they immediately remember and think why. They should ask themselves what is it about it that attracts them— them uniquely. As I said earlier, even the designer may not know it all, and might think some interpretations pretty far-out. But if it works for *users*…

Human minds are unfathomable, fantastic, and incredible in a great way—so why not let them have their full imaginative sway?

And so it seems to be with the Apple logo.

Anyway, by now the love people have built up for Apple devices is inseparable from Apple logo love. If they didn't love Apple devices *and* the Apple logo, they wouldn't put the logo in the rear windows of their cars, would they?

CHAPTER SIX

Growing a designer

L uck, they say.

    So do I, at times.

Like Silicon Valley, 1977—right place, right time, right person. As if that one, lucky moment was the beginning of it all.

I don't think so.

Because (and you *already* know this), don't you help make your own luck?

When people talked about the great golfer Arnold Palmer, and his "lucky" strokes, how did he reply?

"You know, the more I practice, the luckier I get."

Funny how that works out. I am impressed by Matthew Syed's account in his book "Bounce" about how *practicing*, constant practicing, brings luck—

success—to musicians, chess players, everyone. Every mistake I ever made—or design choice that didn't fully succeed—came with the lesson of how to do better next time. Every daunting task that seemed impossible got easier once I started doing it.

Yes, luck did come in. But maybe I'd earned some of that luck.

It's not enough to be at the right place at the right time. You also have to be *ready*—even when you don't know what's coming.

So let me tell you about the lead-up to that single magic moment.

I was born in the Los Angeles suburb of Culver City, into an extended family with more than its share of artists—one uncle was an art director, another a commercial photographer, two cousins were fine artists and another a famous ceramicist. Growing up in the 1950s and '60s, I knew at an early age that my path would lead to working in some creative field. I believed in it because my family always held the arts in such high regard. I'm sure my mom encouraged all my creative endeavors as a kid.

I don't know when I became aware that someone actually created all the ads, messages, and the everyday *look* of things that kids usually take for granted. I do have vivid memories of tagging along with my mom to the supermarket and gazing at the rows of products and all those images—recognizing cereal boxes and food packaging I'd seen on TV. They seemed to be a kind of secret language—all telling a story in their graphics, pictures, colors, and shapes.

Like all kids in the 1950s, I was glued to the TV set, always being told I was sitting too close to it. But the CBS network logo was so amazing to me. It was a big, graphic eye—a clear, crisp image that *represented* something. This was a bit of graphic wit that wasn't over my head: "Here I am watching TV, and here's an eye watching *me*. Isn't that cool?" And, basically, the CBS logo hasn't changed since it was created 70 years ago. *That's* a classic.

By the time I was in high school, I knew my career focus would be on *design* in some form, and San Jose

*The CBS logo as it was, introduced in 1951, and as it is today.
The same basic icon lasted all these years, much like the Apple logo.*

State University in California's Silicon Valley seemed to be the place where everything was happening. With so many artists in our extended family, my father—who had his own successful dry cleaning business—was well aware of the unsteady income that came with a career in art. Because he was footing my college bill, I made a deal with him so he'd agree to let me go away to school. I chose to major in Industrial Design, a field—in his eyes—where I could get a "real" job.

I did well enough, but soon decided I wasn't really enamored with doing renderings of cars and toasters—I missed working with words and ideas. So I soon switched my focus to *Graphic* Design.

Why graphics? Well, as I've said, something like that had already captured my imagination. I'd always been inspired by design legends like Saul Bass, Paul Rand and Milton Glaser. I loved their kind of symbolic simplicity and how much they could say with such clean, bold images. And clearly, there was *fun* to be had playing with words and pictures—especially in all the work that I admired. That was what pushed me into wanting to get into graphics.

College courses in graphic design "back in the day" were not the advanced courses they are today, due in great part to the design revolution that came with the introduction of computers and digital design. Still, they were a great foundation and very worthwhile. In my case though, I seemed to learn so much more while working on the job.

Can anyone become a graphic designer? The short answer is "maybe."

Some skills can be learned, but I think other, more instinctive, talents need to be present in order to become really good. In any creative field, the qualities of imagination, inspiration and intuition are crucial. These can be encouraged to grow—but the seed has to be there. No matter how creative you are, you still need to learn about what others have done, and are doing. Graphic design doesn't exist in a vacuum. There's a cultural conversation going on all the time. The same is true for every other creative field.

So in terms of an education, it pays to open your mind, feel the vibes, look at the world through others' eyes, and learn by hearing others' voices. This way of learning is available to everyone and is helpful in every profession, really, but it's especially important in communication fields. Seeing and listening is what communication is all about!

There are a few skills that are vital to becoming a graphic designer. Some of these skills, though undeveloped, were natural for me from the beginning, but I didn't really have a names for them.

One thing you definitely need is a *good sense of design*. What is a good sense of design? It's having an "eye"—being able to see what's working in a design, and what's not.

Having a good sense of design means you can recognize things in a graphic composition like *balance* and *flow* and the overall *rightness*. It almost becomes an automatic response, to be able to sense what looks "off" in a graphic composition. Are the proportions right? Is one detail upstaging the overall message? Are the color and font choices making the desired statement? These are all things you *feel*. It's where the *art* of design comes into play. Training and experience can help you develop your design sense, but you have to have some instinct for it in order to get really good.

Right up there with design sense, is design *thinking*. Design thinking is first *defining the problem*, then *designing the solution*. That's the most satisfying part about being a graphic designer for me, it's coming up with the "big idea" that solves the graphic problem. It's what separates designs that are just decorative from designs that *say* something.

On many projects, the idea is the most important

element. You can communicate—and sometimes even sell—a strong idea with just a scrawl on the back of a napkin. Variations of how you execute the design idea can follow later, but if it's strong enough, it doesn't depend on execution in order to communicate.

But that does bring up another important aspect to the art of design—which is execution, or *craft*. Attention to detail and nuance matters tremendously, especially in creating something as honed and long-lasting as a logo. All the elements have to be painstakingly finessed for maximum impact—the letter spacing, the size relationships, the flow of a line, the precise tone of a color... every single choice. It all adds up to make a good idea even more powerful.

And, of course, I have to add to this list of skills, traits like *creativity* and *originality*.

I hate to break the news to aspiring young designers, but it's all been done before. The designer's challenge *always* is "What can I do to make my design feel fresh, distinctive or unexpected?" Sometimes it's bold, sometimes it's subtle. It's rarely easy. But that's one of the design problems to solve, isn't it?

Education can only take you so far. I found that my skills and design thinking improved with years of real-work problem solving and collaborating with many talented, seasoned professionals.

After college, I eagerly embarked on a series of jobs at small advertising and design agencies with early hi-tech clients, in rapidly-changing Silicon Valley. I learned so much from working on actual accounts day after day. I kept building my portfolio with better samples of my work, and eventually landed a job at the advertising agency of Regis McKenna in Palo Alto.

That was where it happened. That moment I couldn't see coming—the beginning of a very exciting chapter in my life that influenced everything that followed.

No question about it—being new and working with a startup client that would go on to become one of the most profitable companies in the world was remarkably fortunate. Designing the Apple logo opened a lot of doors for me.

But I'd like to clear up a misconception that people often assume incorrectly—I didn't own the rights to the Apple logo, and I certainly never received royalties for my Apple logo design. That's not how it works. I was never an employee of Apple. I worked for Regis McKenna, glad to have a good job with a pay check every two weeks—like everyone else. Apple was one of our many paying clients—the one who just happened to become the most successful company in the world.

It's amazing to think I've lived through an important part of history, been part of it, even helped to give it a little push! What a difference now.

Back in 1977, when I was introduced to the concept of a "home" computer, I thought only computer professionals would actually do the applications we were promoting in our advertising. You really had to know computer language, programming and how to use the basic software available at the time to do your household finances or keep track of recipes. I certainly didn't use a computer then, but because of where I lived and worked, I was more aware of computers than the average person.

But that was the Apple II. In the very beginning, lack of computer memory was a major weakness. Data for the Apple II was recorded and stored on *audio cassette tapes* called "data cassettes." They were "played" on a portable cassette player/recorder plugged into the Apple II—if you can imagine that. After the Apple logo was approved, my next assignment was designing labels for the data cassettes. In a couple years, the cassette was replaced with a floppy disk that was inserted into a custom disk drive called the Disk II. It solved Apple II's biggest weakness—lack of storage—and was an incredibly profitable innovation for Apple.

The Disk II floppy disk drive for the Apple II helped start the fever for Apple products.

The technology kept changing rapidly. By the mid-80s, the Apple Macintosh appeared on the scene, a real game-changer with a totally different, more advanced operating system—one that didn't need an external drive to input your data. The Mac was *so* much more intuitive for the average user. The difference was like apples and oranges (pardon the pun). The Mac was the gateway to making digital design available and possible for everybody.

Before personal computers, designers, art directors and studio artists created all their layouts and "camera-ready" final art by hand. We drew our designs using draftsman tools—drawing pencils, tracing paper, T-squares, circle templates, French curves, Rapidograph ink pens, and *lots and lots* of color markers. We marked up ad copy to precise specifications, sent it out to typesetting companies to be set, and then it was pasted in place with wax or rubber cement by keyline artists. We marked up acetate overlays on the final art with instructions for printers who separated the colors for 4-color printing. And that's how the Apple logo—and all of Apple's first print work—was created. It wasn't possible any other way... *yet.*

To get on board with the computer revolution, advertising and design agencies first invested in maybe *one* computer, and *one* computer technician. I remember looking over the shoulder of the technician and giving art direction on the finishing touches of my designs.

But in a few short years, those agencies had to fork over the money to supply their entire creative staffs with their *own* computers—and then invest in computer *training* for everyone. I didn't start actually using my own Apple computer for designing until around 1992.

My generation of designers and art directors bridged that quantum leap in how creative work was done— before and after the Mac. Not everyone could make the transition, some found it too overwhelming to relearn everything, and become digital.

But the change was unstoppable. Today, it's essential for a designer to be well-versed in the design software that's available, such as Adobe InDesign, Photoshop, Illustrator and the ever-growing, ever-changing arsenal of capabilities.

Even so—all the design technology is still only a *tool*. It may facilitate the design process and give you countless capabilities to do what used to take many different professionals to do—but it doesn't *make* you a designer.

You still need the idea, the imagination—the *eye*.

But, truthfully, I can't imagine my life without my Macs. This hit me yesterday as I was cooking dinner, leaning over the counter, reading a recipe on the screen. I use my laptop and tablet for everything—graphic design projects, internet communications, presentations, as well as the daily business of life, from calendars to cooking! Portability is the thing for me now. I find myself doing a lot more traveling lately, so I always carry my tablet with me, just to stay on top of it all.

What a blessing. And to think that I was a part of what made Apple what it is today. Awesome!

Me posing with a vintage Mac.
As the Mac became more popular, so did the Apple logo.
(Matt Rodbard/Synk-Ziff Davis)

CHAPTER SEVEN

Bits of history—
Apple's and mine

Because of Apple's rapid growth and success, the world of big business took notice. The company was fast outgrowing our small agency in Palo Alto.

In 1981, Chiat/Day, a big, national, award-winning ad agency headquartered in Los Angeles, bought out Regis McKenna's advertising business—mainly for the purpose of acquiring the Apple account with it. I was the only member of Regis McKenna's creative team who was also acquired by Chiat/Day in the merger—every other creative was let go. I was told it was because we were in the middle of creating Apple's first national TV campaign, and Chiat/Day didn't want to upset Steve. Welcome to the fickle world of big-time advertising!

Suddenly, I had a new employer and I would soon relocate to Chiat/Day's New York office.

Chiat/Day was one of the hottest agencies in the country then. I had always wanted to live and work in New York City—"The Big Apple"—so I was excited and, to be honest, a bit apprehensive. New York was going to be a radical change from my laid-back Californian life.

The new Apple print and TV campaign we had begun at Regis McKenna in Palo Alto, would end up being completed by Chiat/Day in Los Angeles and New York. I was the only common link between the two agencies and the in-progress creative work transferring from one agency to the other—a tough spot to be in.

Before the acquisition, we—the creative team from McKenna—had chosen the TV host Dick Cavett to be the first celebrity spokesperson for Apple. Known for his intelligence and quick wit, Cavett was popular among the young, smart set—famous for his lively interviews with the biggest cultural icons of the time—including David Bowie, Muhammed Ali, Groucho Marx, Marlon Brando, Katherine Hepburn, Jimi Hendrix, John Lennon and Yoko Ono.

The association with Cavett felt right for Apple, which was still developing its brand personality. Cavett's sophistication and his down-to-earth sense of humor

Me with Dick Cavett on the set of the photo shoot for a full-page Apple ad in the Wall Street Journal—a big deal at the time.

(he *is* from Nebraska) reflected well on the smart and confident young company.

By 1981, Apple was ready to position its "personal computer" as something more than just a place to file recipes and track home finances. The Chiat/Day TV work with Cavett promoted the Apple computer as a place to conduct *business* from home, as well as the office—a relatively radical concept for most professions at the time—and taken for granted now, thanks to home computers.

During this transition, I was glad to be expanding my creative skills and opportunities beyond print advertising and graphics alone. But it was difficult to be thrust into an established creative department—with its carefully chosen creatives competing in the fast lane of New York advertising. I had been "acquired" by Chiat/Day to placate Steve, as a part of the company merger—and not really *hired* by anyone. With no allies, I never felt that I was really "one of them"—but more like part of a package deal. Not surprisingly, after about eight months at Chiat/Day, I was laid off. This was my life lesson that political connections in careers can only take you so far—or only so far as you are useful.

It was scary. Making cold call appointments, showing my portfolio up and down New York's famed Madison Avenue—the center of the advertising universe.

I soon found work with other another top New York agency. Having the Apple logo in my portfolio certainly didn't hurt. The clients were big companies with top brands, for cars, liquors, and other glamorous categories. But it was never the fun of the Apple time, when I was talking directly to the person calling the shots. Along with big advertising agencies comes big budgets—and big drama! It was mostly about the bottom line. With the ups and downs of major clients moving their businesses from agency to agency, a lot of creative employees were laid off, and then found work again at other agencies. It came with the territory. All the same, for me it was a great mind-blowing time.

I enjoyed doing some good work for companies like IBM, publisher Simon & Schuster and other global firms. As my experience and responsibilities expanded, I seemed to have been perceived as more of an "advertiser" than a "logo designer," but since it was still all about communication, I was fine with that. I soon realized I was using many of the same skills in advertising as in logo design. Researching a product for advertising projects is not very different from researching a company for branding and logo projects. You look for insights and points of difference. What does the product or company do better than the competition? Who's the target market for the product or company? What message do you want to communicate to that market? Researching gives you answers to these questions, which in turn helps you develop strategic, meaningful creative solutions for your projects.

I was learning a lot and having a great time in New York, the "city that doesn't sleep" because, like the song says, "if you can make it there, you'll make it anywhere…"

After a few years, I got a job offer that promised me the opportunity for even more TV work—which I wanted—in Chicago, another big advertising center. I found Chicago to be a more inviting, more livable city than New York, with plenty of its own brand of excitement, and it's my home now.

During these years of my career, as I was growing and adapting to the changing times, so was the Apple logo.

Apple's first change was in the early '80s. Steve hired Landor Associates, a brand consulting firm in San Francisco, to do a logo revision. They were paid a ton of money and enhanced it slightly—sleeking up the lines and perhaps brightening up the colors for the digital age. Printing technology was changing as fast as the computer revolution that Steve helped create. It's important for companies to keep their icons showing and reproducing at their best. I always thought Landor did a great thing.

Apple's colorful logo worked well in the 1970s when their competitors' computer screens were just black and white. It also helped humanize the brand for home use. The striped version of the Apple logo was the unchanged symbol of the company for 21 years—displayed on every Apple user's screen in homes, schools and offices in cities all over the world.

But times were changing. Apple innovations had become the industry standard. Full color was no longer the differentiator that it had been for Apple—*all* computers now offered vibrant colors on their screens. And everyone was making home computers. Around 1998, Steve decided the colored stripes had served their purpose.

In the 90's, Apple finances were pretty bad and the company was in dire need of business customers' attention—the Mac wasn't just for personal use any longer. So Apple's logo had to convey ideas of durability, stability, professionalism and modernity. Steve wanted to make the logo more serious and neutral. The logo had to keep up with the times.

Apple managed to keep the original logo's "humanity" in their new "3D" one-color versions—the rounded bevel and curved reflections gave the monochromatic logos some extra life. And to carry on Apple's color tradition, the new iMac shells came in a range of bright candy colors.

Apple logo versions keep coming. A crystal version arrived in 2001, and a chrome variant in 2007. Now it's white—which I like for its simplicity.

As you can see, the silhouette of the Apple logo has stayed basically the same even though the coloring and rendering have evolved over time. I'm glad the logo has been able to stay current. Logos need to say different things as they age. I'm just happy it's in such capable hands.

Whatever the evolution of the logo, it still feels like a part of me. In my everyday life, I see it a lot—iPads, iPhones, Macs, store windows, in movies, on TV—

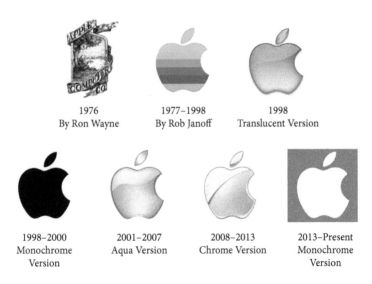

| 1976 | 1977–1998 | 1998 |
| By Ron Wayne | By Rob Janoff | Translucent Version |

| 1998–2000 | 2001–2007 | 2008–2013 | 2013–Present |
| Monochrome Version | Aqua Version | Chrome Version | Monochrome Version |

The Apple logo family tree.

all over. When I walk through an airport and look around, everybody's got their laptops up, and half of them have little white shiny Apples. It makes me feel so much at home. Something I thought of in *my* world transcends language and cultures—and somebody else is interacting with it, in a very personal way, in *their* world.

Logo as art: Apple Store on 5th Avenue in New York; artist Andy Warhol's Apple, 1985; and a neon interpretation in Tokyo, Japan.

Not every designer has a chance to experience that.

I continued to enjoy my work at big advertising agencies in Chicago during the 1980s-90s. It was an exciting, challenging time—creating print and TV campaigns for a wide variety of major brands. I got a kick out of knowing I was part of the history of well-established products and companies that I knew and liked since I was a kid.

But make no mistake—working in high-powered agencies can be stressful at times, a lot of late nights and a lot of frustrations, especially with clients. The excitement of working around so many talented people was the thrilling part, though, and it taught me so much.

One of the huge rewards of working on big accounts with big budgets is that you get to travel to shoot commercials and print ads—to Hollywood, New York, out of the country even. Working on these out-of-town jobs was not all fun and games—it still involved long, sometimes tedious, hours. But what an amazing experience it is to be working with a team of creative professionals and state-of-the-art production facilities to realize *your* vision—on 30 seconds of film.

No matter what the project—a TV spot or a corporate logo—the creative experience of conceiving an idea, making it come to life in some way, and then seeing others enjoy it, can sometimes be worth the agony of getting there.

After about 15 years of working in this fast-paced, high-pressure arena, I was ready for something different. The industry has its ups and downs—usually reflecting changes in the economy. Suddenly budgets tighten and staffs shrink, so the creative work—which still has to get done—tends to get farmed out to freelancers. So I took the knowledge I had gained, and contacts I had made, and went out on my own to become a freelance art director/designer.

Smaller clients meant smaller budgets, so that meant much different kinds of work. The projects were less elaborate and involved fewer people than the big out-of-town location shooting projects of years before. But that also meant less headaches and a lot more time for "a life."

After a career with big US agencies, I adapted well to the change, even to the new skills it required. Becoming my own businessman was new to me. I was used to—and much preferred—focusing on the creative work and letting big accounting departments and production managers do all the number-crunching. Now instead of getting a regular, bi-weekly paycheck, I got paid only when I delivered finished work. That took a little getting used to.

One thing I was not expecting was the stock market crash of 2008—few people were. The sudden, big drop in the economy, which had a global impact, more or less wiped out my clients, their budgets, and my freelance business. I spent several months trying to figure out what I wanted to do next with my career. Should I—could I—hang it up, coast for a while, and see what new opportunities come up?

And sure enough, something did show up that changed everything—again.

CHAPTER EIGHT

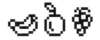

Bearing new fruit

Steve Jobs certainly was a life-changing person in my life and career. But I'm happy to report, he wasn't my only life-changing encounter.

About 10 years ago, I met a man from Australia named Joel who said he really liked my work, but that my web presence "could use some help." The truth is, I knew my website sucked because I hadn't put any effort into it. Anyway, Joel said he wanted to help me develop something for the web, a portfolio site, an e-commerce site… or *whatever.*

Well, that "whatever" turned into a partnership that grew into our own international logo design and branding agency—the Rob Janoff Studio.

Joel made me aware of the great affection for the Apple logo—and for American branding in general—around the world. There are so many companies in other countries wanting to rebrand themselves for the new global market. The fit of their needs and my experience was a perfect match, which I hadn't considered or pursued.

It wasn't long before I was working with a wide range of clients, from many different countries.

Sometimes I have to catch my breath and take a moment to realize what a long, strange trip this career path has been! I never dreamed I would be enjoying my work and my life so much at this point.

The most rewarding part is that I get to meet and work with so many fascinating people via messaging apps like Skype and WeChat—from all over the world. Many are entrepreneurs with new startup companies, filled with excitement about their new "baby." I find it so satisfying to give birth to a new company's brand identity.

Many times my team and I are designing for established companies that need to buff up their brand image, so we talk at length to business owners—sometimes with translators—to figure out how to make their brands come alive again.

Hearing my clients' voices and "meeting" them on the screen, or in person, has been an unexpected bonus of working with international clients. Such a richness of new cultures to learn from! The design challenges are often the same—but also different. Each client and culture has its own unique set of issues in the marketplace. It's important to gain insight into those cultures and understand those issues.

Sometimes, the communication has to speak to a global market and work across borders—just as Apple did, and continues to do. It's so much easier now with technology bringing the world together.

The only "downside" of this new venture for me is adapting to the time changes across the planet. My *evening* may be my client's *morning*—and vice versa—so coordinating life, and sleep, is an ongoing challenge. But what a small price to pay in exchange for such great, interesting clients! My work is never dull.

I'd like to tell you about just a few of the international branding projects my team and I have been working on at the Rob Janoff Studio over the past few years. Perhaps it will give you some idea of the thinking involved in the creative process of branding and graphic design.

Crooz — Our first digital gaming project, and our first client from Tokyo, Japan.

At our initial "meet & greet" in San Francisco, I heard the young, dynamic chairman, Mr. Obuchi, tell the story behind the company name "CROOZ." The poetic CEO saw his company as a "giant ship," and the people who worked there as "crew members"—all working together, traveling across a "water planet" to reach the same destination.

I'll never forget our first live presentation at their top-floor headquarters, with all of vibrant Tokyo below me. I entered the large open work area to the sound of 500 employees giving me a standing ovation. As you can imagine, I was speechless! Being speechless is not a good thing when you are about to give a new client their first look at your new work.

We must have gone through three rounds of concept presentations before they settled on one design. The final choice featured a water drop that formed the letter "C." When we added a small droplet sphere next to the "C," it created a sense of outer space. And what's more, the Crooz logo itself suddenly seemed like a game!

Pluit City — A rebranding project from a major real estate development company in Jakarta, Indonesia.

The company's first assignment for us was to rebrand their corporate identity. That went so well, they then asked us to rebrand a city—built from scratch! Pluit City is an ecologically engineered, upscale, man-made island-city in the Jakarta Bay—designed for living, working and recreation. Their existing logo design, created 2 years earlier, was not grabbing the attention of the Chinese investors they were targeting in their marketing efforts. That initial design for Pluit City was an abstract circular icon, faceted to represent the many diverse activities the new city offered. Perhaps the idea behind that logo wasn't singular enough to make an impression.

During our initial interview with the client, they kept emphasizing the word "luxury" and visually referencing luxury car brands—like Mercedes Benz—that they thought represented the kind of luxury this target would respond to. We settled on the idea of illustrating the island's most representative features, the skyline and the water of the ocean. We created them as if they were gold jewelry, or a medallion on a car. To attract Asian investors, red and gold became the primary color palette. The icon illustrates a shimmering city on the water—and also serves as a terrific branding device that can be used in a decorative pattern to reinforce Pluit City's unique identity.

Langone — This startup cosmetics company in Rome, Italy wanted to launch a new high-end line of organic skin products.

First, we joined the owner's initials, "W" and "L" (for Walter Langone), to design a stylishly simple crown icon, and combined it with his name to create an elegant logo. Then, to establish Langone as a premium cosmetic brand made from organic ingredients, we designed Langone's packaging to differentiate it from other natural product lines. We avoided the typical green and brown color palette associated with competitive natural products. Instead, we created a graphic pattern of black botanical silhouettes set against white and gold—an organically elegant solution.

Hearing Others' Voices

Hearing Others' Voices — A book series intended for young adults, published in London, England.

The very book you are reading now is part of a series for young people to help them track their passions and interests—and project themselves into the future with possible career paths. This icon can be interpreted in multiple ways—it represents people listening to each other, human interconnection and the exchange of ideas. The mark is also reminiscent of ancient hieroglyphics— which you might think of as some of our earliest logos!

After going through our process of creating a new branding identity—the insightful interview questions, the presentation of logo options, discussing the merits of each design choice, and, of course, the face-to-face Skype chats—publisher Ruth Finnegan was so delighted with the experience, she announced that I should write the next book in the series. And here we are!

That's what I love about meeting fascinating clients from all over the world. You never know where they will take you.

∬ rob janoff

RobJanoff.com — This is the current rebranding of our own design firm.

As our business began to take off, it became clear that we could make our own brand more effective and up-to-date. The choice of all lower case letters for my name reflects the more casual, personal nature of our client interaction—without all the formal corporate layers. The design of the icon originated as a graphic representation of a lower case "r" and "j." (My initials, see them?)

At the same time, it represents a continuum—and a collaboration—among our team and with our clients. The many colors in the icon hint at the original, striped Apple logo—the project that made everything that followed for me possible.

Exciting new opportunities continue to arise.

In 2018, I hosted a master class in New York City in collaboration with Fiverr—an online marketplace for creative services—to a live audience in a New York theater which was simultaneously streamed online to a community of over 2 million professional designers and freelance artists worldwide. My involvement included a promotional contest for a new custom logo—designed by me and my team—which would go to three lucky companies who wrote in, describing their business and why they wanted a new logo. Hundreds of entries arrived in a few days. The response was overwhelming—and so was the process of choosing winners.

What a fun, unusual experience—being able to pick and choose clients we wanted to work with, for a variety of reasons. When I came across the J. Michael Bishop Institute for Cancer Research in Chengdu, China, I was fascinated with their work—combining traditional Chinese herbal medicine with western biological cancer research. It looked like something I wanted to be a part of. Creating graphics for good is particularly appealing at this point in my career, and cross-cultural exchange has never been more important. It's was an honor to see our new logo as a part of the inauguration of the Institute's new offices, in a newly developed complex in Chengdu called Biotown—a campus dedicated to scientific research and discovery.

By the way, I'm happy to report that many of the companies that didn't win the contest, decided to become clients on their own.

Companies that seek me out to create a new logo— or rebrand their existing company—already appreciate the importance of good branding. The success of Apple and its logo made *everybody* more brand-conscious.

In the process of developing a brand identity for an entrepreneur and his or her new company, I get to learn a lot about them and their business. Lots of questions... How do you see your company out in the marketplace? What kind of personality do you want your company to project? Of course, it isn't just the details of the specific business that I need to hear about, it's also the context in which they are working and the obstacles and constraints they face.

We keep on probing so we can graphically communicate that feeling in a logo. And it's a great way to get to know new clients—so easy now through emails and Skype.

The internet has opened the doors to incredible business opportunities—it's certainly the great revolutionary development of our time. Unimaginable when I started. It has made the world smaller, and enabled the sharing of everything—with everybody—possible.

However, that capability has consequences we haven't quite learned how to manage yet—including artists and designers. Evaluating the work we do is subjective. Just because everyone has an opinion doesn't give those opinions equal value.

Filtering legitimate critiques from baseless criticism can be an exhausting task for even the most seasoned professionals. If you're an aspiring designer, don't let this drive you away. Young people especially put a lot of care, and a lot of love, into whatever they create, and when they get harsh criticism, it's a crusher.

I spend a lot of time talking about how this criticism is not about you. You rarely hear, "I like you, but this piece you did has these things I don't like, and here's why". Some stranger on the internet isn't going to bother with those distinctions, or think that, or care really, because they don't care what people think. I care a lot about designers and what designers think—especially from teaching them.

In this digital age—for better or worse—graphic design and computer skills have become inseparable. This isn't to say that beautiful designs and calligraphy aren't still being created they way they have been for millennia—by hand. But the high-speed nature of today's working world demands digital capabilities—even if it's just to enhance hand-created art, take it to a new level, or transmit and reproduce it anywhere in the world.

I personally think, though, that if left unchecked, the technical implementation of a solution can sometimes get in the way of the creative process. When I'm talking to young people, I see the tendency to go straight to the computer—but, often, that's devoid of an idea.

Sometimes tech can be an idea-killer, because you're spending all your time on making that corner perfect, or fussing over some other digital detail, and you're forgetting what the bigger picture is—what the bigger *idea* is.

Everyone has his or her own creative process, but in my opinion, the concept—a solid idea—should come first, and the execution should follow.

I am sometimes asked if there are any logos out there that I would like to have done myself.

Yes! Of course!

Can you see the hidden arrow?

I always like to mention two classic logos that inspired me.

The FedEx logo. It is brilliant. They went into a market dominated by United Parcel Service, or UPS, with its brown trucks and tasteful little gold logo. And instead, FedEx—or Federal Express—had white trucks with a *huge*, bold, orange and blue logo. FedEx did everything the opposite of UPS so it would stand out—which was one of the designer's main goals.

And symbolically (and subliminally) the logo tells you exactly what FedEx does with that secret arrow between the "E" and the "X"—it's a courier firm that gets your package from *here* to *there*.

That's the interactive wit I like to encourage whenever

possible. I love the way its straightforwardness—five blocky letters pressed together, shifting from deep blue to orange—lead into the realization that there's an arrow hidden in the negative space. I love a logo that gives you a surprise. You go, "Oh, I get it!" The meaning of the whole service is in that secret little arrow.

I also really like Milton Glaser's "I love New York" logo concept. You know, it was one of the first popular uses of an emoji, though nobody called it that back then. "I ❤ N Y" predates the popular use of texting shorthand by about 25 years!

New Yorkers really do love New York, so the logo struck a chord with its audience—and the rest of the world. The icon is still a big seller on T-shirts, hats and mugs all over New York City. Legend has it that Glaser

Emoji as logo.

came up with the idea while riding in the back of a cab. Now, of course, his design has become part of the universal language.

The online definition of *logo* is "a graphic representation or symbol of a company name, trademark, abbreviation, etc., often uniquely designed for ready recognition."

Even though the word "logo"—a shortened form of *logotype*—originated around 1810, the thing itself, a *graphic representation*, has a history as old as civilization.

Think, for example, of emblems, coats of arms, heraldic devices, flags, decorative initials on spoons and heirlooms, pottery marks, religious icons and calligraphy, ancient shop signs, publishers' marks, watermarks, silver hallmarks, society badges and family crests. And then look at the text-based forms of slogans, mottos, samplers, decorative names on buildings, book covers, and so on, and so on, over the centuries.

Logos can be just words (a wordmark), or just

Well-known brands that need no words
to communicate who they are.

images (a logomark), or both combined. A logo doesn't necessarily have to have *both* an image and a wordmark. Think of Starbucks, McDonalds, and Nike… all brands that started as a combination logo — icon plus workmark. When a dominant icon for a brand identity becomes familiar enough with the public, it can stand alone. That's what happened with Apple in a very short time. A strong icon that can stand alone and still communicate the brand identity is especially valuable for reaching across a global market—no words or translations required!

What could communicate more simply than that?

CHAPTER NINE

New growth

I'm often asked what advice I would give young designers today about the features of a well-designed logo.

There's no recipe for a good logo. I can only offer guidelines—not rules. I suppose one could say that a good logo is one that is remembered. (That would mean, of course, that the bad ones are the just forgotten.) But that's not entirely true.

Maybe it's more accurate to say a successful logo reflects the unique identity of a brand—its personality—in a way that *connects* with people. And a well-designed logo helps that connection.

On that score, I can offer some tips that work for me.

Simplicity

That is what I always begin with, it is essential—the complex art of keeping it simple. Never forget the Golden Rule: "*When in doubt, leave it out.*"

That's what makes a logo stand out—its simplicity.

So many clients want the sun and the moon in their logo, or are obsessed with literalness. They come with laundry lists of elements the logo *must have.* This is a recipe for failure. I have to show those people how a clear message is singular and memorable. I always respond, as you should too, by bringing out the importance—the power—of keeping it simple.

But simple is deceptively difficult.

Logos also need to be distinctive. And if there is a "message" to be gotten across it needs to be visualized *metaphorically*, perhaps subliminally, certainly not literally.

Young designers tend to want to put everything they have into it. That is understandable, but it is usually too much. Simpler things have more impact and are easier to remember.

The Apple logo was just that. It was seen on the corner of every screen of every Apple device, and people remembered it. That is how it has become an internationally known, remembered and loved icon. It is so simple.

Do your homework—
learn everything about your clients

Get all the information you possibly can from and about your clients—this is another absolute essential.

How can you design effectively for a client's product or business without knowing all about it, its competition and the marketplace it exists in? In what context will the consumer see its branding? In a store aisle? On a store sign? On a website? Will you look like everyone else—or will you stand out? What makes your client different and better? Who are you communicating to? Who needs your product? Young people? Business people? Men? Women? Gamers?

And what history does your client have with customers? Can you keep existing customers and also attract new ones?

Sometimes houses get a stale odor, but the owners don't notice. A company's brand can be the same: it sours, yet they seem oblivious. This is where you can discover how they would really like to see themselves, and help them to present themselves like *that*. You can't capture a company's personality without knowing it.

You need more than just information and understanding, though, of course, they are essential parts of the creative process. I believe that you also need *empathy* to reach the right, unique, design solution—empathy for the client and the consumer. Without that it's hard to connect.

As an observer and listener, you may end up having greater insight into your clients' businesses than they have themselves. And, if you do your homework, you should have insight into the consumer as well.

Don't let passing design trends distract you from the core message

Remember that though logo styles change with the times, your first priority should be to maintain your client's vision.

Trendy styles may be cool in the short term, but in time they will date your message and distract from your client's relevance.

The silhouette of the Apple logo has stayed basically

the same for decades, which pleases me. The key message remained, but the coloring and rendering have changed with the times. Currently the trend is toward simplification. Who knows what tomorrow's trend will be?

Typography is one area to watch. Many fonts fall in and out of fashion. I try to stay away from fonts that might date, or that look so flashy or interesting that they take away from other imagery. When I look back at the very first font I used with Apple—it was trendy and looked kind of futuristic—and I wouldn't use it now. I think typography is best when you feel it, but it doesn't get in the way—it affects you, but you don't *consciously* see it.

The right product and branding can lead to business success. So design for the long term. It's much better to refresh—when needed—than to have to rebrand.

Logos are meant to last.

Keep it balanced and alive

Basic principles of design—like balance, cohesion, legibility and emphasis apply to logo design just as they do to a page layout. Try to imagine that your new logo is in a page layout or on a webpage. Does the logo hold together as unit? When you create a great image in your mind or on your screen, you should make it a rule to check out how it works in its environment. Are the different elements in a pleasing proportion to one another? How is the flow? Is the most important element the thing that stands out?

Remember too that most people start looking or reading from the upper left corner and end up in the lower right. So make sure your design makes it easy for your audience to get your intended message.

Spacing, proportion, weight and color are all variables where every nuance matters *tremendously*—especially for a logo that has to work as well on a tiny button as on a huge billboard. Even the space *around* your logo helps hold it together. Play with the choices and test all the applications until everything about your logo design feels *inevitable*—and just right.

Try, if you can, for a wink and a smile in the logo

By "a wink and a smile," I mean something we leave for the consumer to get. It's like saying, as a wink does,

"Here's something just between you and me!" That can cement the relationship between your company's logo and its audience—it turns it into something *personal*.

That's because you remember something that made you smile. Any time you can add some kind of humor— still keeping it simple—it becomes a note of distinction, more likable and memorable. So if you have a sense of humor, *cultivate* it. Wit can come *visually* as well as in words or actions. It's one of the things I like best about graphic design.

Then ask yourself this question. Is the logo *interactive* even when it's not on an interactive device?

Humor may not always be appropriate in every case, but involvement and interaction is.

Any design that invites you to see *into* it, is interactive.

Keep learning, looking, visualizing

If you love graphic design, then live it, breathe it and practice, practice, practice. Theory is fine, but seeing and doing is everything.

Learn from the visual wonders around you, watch people, nature, creatures of the world, look at beautiful colors and shapes and fonts, steep yourself in the human art of the past and present. Keep trying to translate what you see or read into a figurative design in your mind, on paper, in dream. How would you represent *that*—as simply as possible?

All knowledge is power. Seeing how graphic design has developed from cave drawing to digital design is fascinating. As you train in digital software—non-existent when I first started, but unavoidable now—take care not to lose the human touch and feel. There's always been a human connection to symbols—it's in our DNA. Seeing the development of classic designs tells you so much about the culture and graphic trends of the time. This can also spark an idea that might inspire whatever design project you are working on today.

Learning the principles is important. I studied graphic design at a university, and I think things have worked out pretty well. But go on learning wherever you can. Never imagine that you know it all—especially in the ever-changing tech world we live in.

Branding is about visual *communication*. So pay attention to your visuals, but don't lose sight of what you're communicating.

Be clear. Be simple. *Connect.*

The rewards

Beyond my fascination with fonts, shapes, software, and trends, for me the most rewarding part of being a designer is still that magic moment—*arriving at a solution.*

Of course, the satisfaction of finding a solution only comes after a lot of thought-processing—listening to what a client is saying, and what they're *not* saying, and distilling that into a succinct message. Then the problem-solving process of translating that message into an icon begins!

When I started out and chose a path to follow for my life's career, I chose the field of graphic design. I loved solving graphic design problems. It didn't matter if it was an ad, a poster or a logo.

It just so happened that when I problem-solved for a young, visionary client back in Palo Alto in 1977, I had the *incredible* good fortune of seeing my solution take on a life of its own. I watched it become an icon for the world—and for our time in history.

Artists have always created human connections that business and politics cannot. At its best, graphic design has a way of transcending divides of countries and languages. It may originate from business purposes, but when it all comes together, it has the amazing capacity to resonate across cultures and bring people together.

And so the process goes on—with new logos being created by young designers for today.

Now it's *your* turn to solve.

And to grow.

And to watch the world grow with you.

Acknowledgments

First, I want to thank the terrific team I get to work with at Rob Janoff Studio in Australia. I am especially grateful to our company's CEO, Joel Bohm. Joel's friendship and encouragement opened a door to a whole new world of global corporate identity design and branding. For his super sharp business acumen and his devotion to making our business a success, I will be forever grateful. I want to thank our creative director, Andy Koch, for his creatively fertile mind, meticulous attention to detail, tireless work ethic and for being such a joy to collaborate with.

A *most* appreciative "thank you" goes to author and anthropologist Professor Ruth Finnegan, FBA, for making this book possible. Without her support through Balestier Press, her enthusiasm, and her providing the framework and inspiration for this book, it would not have happened.

Our publishers Ruth Finnegan and Roh-Suan Tung of Balestier Press.

Rob Janoff Studio was fortunate to be chosen to rebrand the logo for Ruth's *Hearing Others' Voices* series—a volume of which you are reading this very minute. To learn about her company, my team and I talked in depth with Ruth and the editors by email, phone and Skype. Ruth said afterwards, "I felt that you saw into my soul and drew out things I hadn't ever realized myself." I could say the same to Ruth. I am pleased that our design graces her wonderful series.

Finally, I want to thank my husband, Ed Zimkus, for his writing and editing talents on this book, and for being a second pair of eyes on this and other projects. Thank you, most of all, for your love and support over the past two decades.

Designing for good

It is always satisfying to be able to support a very worthy cause by contributing something I enjoy doing—designing.

The following logo designs were created by our team for these charities and programs in the past few years.

J. Michael Bishop Institute For Cancer Research, *Chengdu, China* — It's no coincidence that the institute is located in Chengdu, the most ideal location in the world for harvesting and processing the herbs used in traditional Chinese medicine. Combined with the most advanced western biological research on cancer pioneered by the Nobel Prize winner, J. Michael Bishop, the institute is leading the charge in fighting the global war against cancer and eradicating one of the world's deadliest diseases.

Sarraf Strata / Camp Quality, *Sydney, Australia* — Sarraf Strata is a property development and management company owned by Norman Sarraf, who is a major contributor to—as well as chairman of—the Camp Quality board of directors. Camp Quality provides innovative programs and services to families of kids fighting cancer. Because of his enthusiastic support of such a worthy cause, we were especially happy to help Norman rebrand his company with a redesign of the Sarraf Strata logo (not the Camp Quality logo above)—just as we're glad to contribute a percentage of the proceeds from all our work in Australia to Camp Quality.

Lucas / LitterGram, *UK* — Danny Lucas (who's a big fan of Apple and the logo) is president of a family-owned business in large-scale commercial fit-out and finish building projects—which include the landmark London Shard and 2012 Olympic venues. Over the years, the company accumulated other related businesses, all with different names and looks. Our successful rebranding put them all under the redesigned Lucas name, giving cohesion to its many branches with a unified look.

After becoming frustrated by the continued accumulation of litter covering the beautiful countryside near London, Danny came back to us to help him with his crusade to fight litter. We created a logo for LitterGram, a campaign using social media to post photos and draw attention to how much retail litter blights the countryside. The photos clearly show the tossed retail logos for everyone to see—which helps create the intended social media buzz.

More things you might like

Internet links

youtube.com/watch?v=dZlsq4N-75k

youtube.com/watch?v=Bauln9ZF_qs

youtube.com/watch?v=UL5h-Umk1Vc

youtube.com/watch?v=ixcJ7cGVJlQ

Books

David Airey, *Logo Design Love: A Guide to Creating Iconic Brand Identities*, New Riders, 2010

Beryl McAlhone, David Staurt, Greg Quinton, Nick Asbury, *A Smile in the Mind*, Phaidon Press, 2016

Alina Wheeler, *Designing Brand Identity: An Essential Guide for the Whole Branding Team*, Wiley, 2017

Ruth Finnegan, *Communicating: The Multiple Modes of Human Interconnection*, Routledge, 2013

Questions for discussion, reflection and action

1. How would you interpret the *Hearing Others'
   Voices* logo on this book's cover (and elsewhere)?
   Why? What's your best friend's interpretation? If
   you differ, can you reflect on why this might be?

2. Having now read this book, which logo option
   (*from all 6 above*) would you have chosen? As
   yourself? As the client/publisher, *Hearing Others'
   Voices*? Why? And for what purpose?

3. Try designing a different logo for *Hearing Others' Voices*. What considerations did you need to consider?

4. Then do the same for yourself, or some cause you are identified with (or, a sports team, church, family, music group…).

5. What is your favorite logo? Why? (Try explaining why to a friend.)

6. What is your favorite work of art, or picture? Why? Does this have anything in common with your logo preferences?

7. Debate the question of whether—and how far— logo designers should study the history of art.

8. Make up a fictional company and imagine you and a friend are representatives of that company. Think about how the logo for this imagined company should look. What does it need to communicate? Set up a debate and argue for your contending logo choices. What might you learn from these points of view?

9. Look at the logo icon on the home page of callenderpress.co.uk. What is it? What do you think of it? How well does it match the Callender Press aims? What does it seem to symbolize? What are its associations? After that, but only after that, scroll down to see the Callender Press perspective on it. Interesting?

10. Repeat the above process with some other logo you admire and/or with one of your own creation (ask others as well as yourself). Do you think such symbolisms matter?

11. What do you think luck has to do with happenings in your life? Your best friend's? A graphic designer's?

Follow us on social media @HearingOthers

HearingOthers

HearingOthers

HearingOthers

Hearing Others' Voices

Hearing Others' Voices is a transcultural and transdisciplinary book series in simple and straightforward language—to inform and engage general readers, undergraduates and, above all, sixth formers (high schoolers in America) in recent advances in thought, unaccountably overlooked areas of the world, and key issues of the day.

CPSIA information can be obtained
at www.ICGtesting.com
Printed in the USA
BVHW090347231020
591518BV00005B/250

9 781911 221616